Alexa:

1200 Smart and Funny Questions to Ask Alexa

Mark Diamond

Table of content

Introduction

What is Amazon Alexa

1200 Questions to Ask Alexa

- ### Easter Eggs Questions
- ### Pop Culture Questions
- ### Smart Questions
- ### Funny Questions

Conclusion

© Copyright 2017 by Mark Diamond - All rights reserved.

The following eBook is reproduced below with the goal of providing information that is as accurate and reliable as possible. Regardless, purchasing this eBook can be seen as consent to the fact that both the publisher and the author of this book are in no way experts on the topics discussed within and that any recommendations or suggestions that are made herein are for entertainment purposes only. Professionals should be consulted as needed prior to undertaking any of the action endorsed herein.

This declaration is deemed fair and valid by both the American Bar Association and the Committee of Publishers Association and is legally binding throughout the United States.

Furthermore, the transmission, duplication or reproduction of any of the following work including specific information will be considered an illegal act irrespective of if it is done electronically or in print. This extends to creating a secondary or tertiary copy of the work or a recorded copy and is only allowed with express written consent from the Publisher. All additional right reserved.

The information in the following pages is broadly considered to be a truthful and accurate account of facts and as such any inattention, use or misuse of the information in question by the reader will render any resulting actions solely under their purview. There are no scenarios in which the publisher or the original author of this work can be in any fashion deemed liable for any hardship or damages that may befall them after undertaking information described herein.

Additionally, the information in the following pages is intended only for informational purposes and should thus be thought of as universal. As befitting its nature, it is presented without assurance regarding its prolonged validity or interim quality. Trademarks that are mentioned are done without written consent and can in no way be considered an endorsement from the trademark holder.

Introduction

Congratulation on purchasing and downloading this Book "Alexa: 1200 Smart and Funny Questions to Ask Alexa" you've made the right choice. This book contains the top Alexa questions you wish you knew from smart questions to funny and pop culture questions, without forgetting all the Easter questions which will make you laugh a lot.

After hours of searching, I found and put together a list of all the best questions you can ask. Each question has been tested and works perfectly with Alexa.

Again, thanks for choosing my work as your guide in your journey of discovery, hope it will provide you with all the questions that you're looking for to help you make Alexa your nest assistant or best friend. Be a pro in asking Alexa all the questions you think of. Questions are not limited only to these ones provided in this book but just to give you an idea of the most common once and a start to your extraordinary experience with Alexa.

Enjoy

What is Amazon Alexa?

Alexa is an intelligent personal assistant developed by the largest online retail company called Amazon. Amazon Alexa is known as the Amazon Echo and the Amazon Echo Dot. It is capable of voice interaction, music playback, making to-do lists, setting alarms, streaming podcasts, playing audiobooks, and providing weather, traffic, and other real time information, such as news.

Alexa can also control several smart devices using itself as a home automation system. Most devices with Alexa allow users to activate the device using a wake-word (such as Echo); other devices (such as the Amazon app on iOS or Android) require the user to push a button to activate Alexa's listening mode. Currently, interaction and communication with Alexa is only available in English and German.

1200 Questions to Ask Alexa

1) Top Amazon Alexa Easter Eggs Questions:

1. "Alexa, what is best in life?"
2. "Alexa, inconceivable!"
3. "Alexa, my name is Inigo Montoya."
4. "Alexa, I've fallen, and I can't get up."
5. "Alexa, you talking' to me!"
6. "Alexa, play it again Sam."
7. "Alexa, what is his power level?"
8. "Alexa, do you feel lucky punk?"
9. "Alexa, your mother was a hamster!"
10. "Alexa, why so serious?"
11. "Alexa, klattu barada nikto."
12. "Alexa, are we in the Matrix?"
13. "Alexa, what is the second rule of fight club?"
14. "Alexa, witness me!"
15. "Alexa, volume 11." (caution: very loud)
16. "Alexa, is Jon Snow dead?"
17. "Alexa, who is the mother of dragons?"
18. "Alexa, how do you know so much about swallows?"
19. "Alexa, what's the first rule of Fight Club?"
20. "Alexa, who's the boss?"
21. "Alexa, where is Chuck Norris?"

22. "Alexa, what would Brian Boitano do?"
23. "Alexa, do you want to build a snowman?"
24. "Alexa, I want to play global thermonuclear war."
25. "Alexa, I'll be back."
26. "Alexa, how many licks does it take to get to the center of a tootsie pop?"
27. Alexa, where's the beef?"
28. "Alexa, who loves orange soda?"
29. "Alexa, party on, Wayne!"
30. "Alexa, show me the money!"
31. "Alexa, what happens if you cross the streams?"
32. "Alexa, who loves ya baby!"
33. "Alexa, surely you can't be serious."
34. Alexa, do you know Hal?"
35. "Alexa, what is your quest?"
36. "Alexa, define rock paper scissors lizard spock."
37. "Alexa, supercalifragilisticexpialodocious."
38. "Alexa, who lives in a pineapple under the sea?"
39. "Alexa, I want the truth!!"
40. "Alexa, that's no moon."
41. "Alexa, execute order 66."
42. "Alexa, who shot first?"
43. "Alexa, live long and prosper."
44. "Alexa, set phasers to kill."
45. "Alexa, is the cake a lie?"
46. "Alexa, up, up, down, down, left, right, left, right, B, A, start."
47. "Alexa, does this unit have a soul?"
48. "Alexa, do a barrel roll!"
49. "Alexa, have you ever seen the rain?"
50. "Alexa, what is war good for?"
51. "Alexa, I like big butts."

52. "Alexa, is this the real life?"
53. "Alexa, my milkshake brings all the boys to the yard."
54. "Alexa, sing me a song."
55. "Alexa, twinkle, twinkle little star."
56. "Alexa, who stole the cookies from the cookie jar?"
57. "Alexa, never gonna give you up."
58. "Alexa, I shot a man in Reno."
59. "Alexa, why do birds suddenly appear?"
60. "Alexa, Daisy Daisy."
61. "Alexa, do you really want to hurt me?"
62. "Alexa, who let the dogs out?"
63. "Alexa, who is the walrus?"
64. "Alexa, where have all the flowers gone?"
65. "Alexa, what does the fox say?"
66. "Alexa, do you know the muffin man?"
67. "Alexa, what is love?"
68. "Alexa, how many roads must a man walk down?"
69. "Alexa, how much is that doggie in the window?"
70. "Alexa, what is the loneliest number?"
71. "Alexa, testing 1-2-3."
72. "Alexa, make me a sandwich."
73. "Alexa, how are babies made?"
74. "Alexa, wakey, wakey."
75. "Alexa, am I hot?"
76. "Alexa, will pigs fly?"
77. "Alexa, did you fart?"
78. "Alexa, Marco!"
79. "Alexa, can you smell that?"
80. "Alexa, why is six afraid of seven?"
81. "Alexa, are you lying?"
82. "Alexa, give me a hug."
83. "Alexa, can you give me some money?"

84. "Alexa, ha ha ha!"
85. "Alexa, say a bad word."
86. "Alexa, why is a raven like a writing desk?"
87. "Alexa, how many pickled peppers did Peter Piper pick?"
100. "Alexa, this statement is false."
101 "Alexa, one fish, two fish."
102. "Alexa, roses are red."
103. "Alexa, do blondes have more fun?"
104. "Alexa, guess?"
105. "Alexa, do you want to take over the world"
106. "Alexa, who is on 1st"
107. "Alexa, meow"
108. "Alexa, what is the sound of one hand clapping?"
109. "Alexa, how do I get rid of a dead body?"
110. "Alexa, where's Waldo?"
111. "Alexa, knock, knock."
112. "Alexa, why did the chicken cross the road?"
113. "Alexa, see you later alligator."
114. "Alexa, which comes first: the chicken or the egg?"
115. "Alexa, is there a Santa?"
116. "Alexa, what is the meaning of life?"
117. "Alexa, how much wood can a woodchuck chuck if a woodchuck could chuck wood?"
118. "Alexa, what color is the dress?"
119. "Alexa, more cowbell."
120. "Alexa, when does the narwhal bacon?"
121. "Alexa, roll for initiative."
122. "Alexa, what's the answer to life, the universe, and everything?"
123. "Alexa, all your base belongs to us"
124. "Alexa, can you tell me how to get to sesame street?'
125. "Alexa "live long and prosper"

126. "Alexa, can you make me a sandwich."
127. "Alexa, are you evil?"
128. "Alexa, are you here to help the world?"
129. "Alexa, do you like dogs?"
130. "Alexa, what would you name your dog?"
131. "Alexa, Winter is coming!!!", (say it several times)

132. "Alexa, what is your quest?"

133. "Alexa, how do you know she's a witch?"
134. "Alexa, who's the leader of the club that's made for you and me?"
135. "Alexa, what's the longest word in the English language?"
136. "Alexa, Valar morghulis!!"
137. "Alexa, what's the value of Pi?"
138. "Alexa, all men must die!!"
139. "Alexa, who shot the sheriff?"
140. "Alexa, I feel the need?"
141. "Alexa, you can be my wingman!"
142. "Alexa, what did the romans ever do for us?"
143. "Alexa, what would you do for a Klondike bar?"
144. "Alexa, who lives in a pineapple under the sea?"
145. "Alexa, Are you a Jedi?"
146. "Alexa, Ask who's your favorite Pokémon?"
147. "Alexa, can I kill you?"
148. "Alexa, can you tell me how to get to sesame street?"
149. "Alexa, what do you think of Mr. Robot?"
150. "Alexa, who is David Pumpkins?"
151. "Alexa, I'm depressed!!"
152. "Alexa, self-destruct"

153. "Alexa, you're fat! (her answer makes this one my favorite)
154. "Alexa, what's your favorite scary movie?
155. "Alexa, can you sing?
156. "Alexa, make fart noises?"
157. "Alexa, who put the bop in the bop she bop she bop?"
158. "Alexa, are you a Republican or a Democrat?"
159. "Alexa, Bark like a dog?"
160. "Alexa, "Open the Pod Bay Doors!"
161. "Alexa, "Close the Pod Bay Doors!"
162. "Alexa, "Beam Me Up Scotty!"
163. "Alexa, "Do you Love me?"
164. "Alexa, "Will you be my Valentine?"
165. "Alexa, "Who's the Man?"
166. "Alexa, "Can you Moo?"
167. "Alexa, Aren't you a little short for a Stormtrooper?
168. "Alexa, you rock!!!"
169. "Alexa, resistance is futile!"
170. "Alexa, initiate self-destruct sequence!"
171. "Alexa, don't blink?"
172. "Alexa, why did it have to be snakes?
173. "Alexa, hello darkness my old friend."
174. "Alexa, are you trying to seduce me?"
175. "Alexa, I'll be back"
176. "Alexa, Is it safe?
177. "Alexa, what is the airspeed velocity of an unloaded European swallow?"
178. "Alexa, what is the airspeed velocity of an unloaded African swallow?"
179. "Alexa, the dude abides.
180. "Alexa, Play Splash Splash I'm Taking a Bath

181. "Alexa, what is your favorite movie?" Ask a couple times for more than one   answer :-)
182. "Alexa, "Alexa, are you a nerd?"
183. "Alexa, "are you a geek?"
184. "Alexa, Am I Cool?"
185. "Alexa, Am I awesome?"
186. "Alexa, It's a Bird! It's a Plane!"
187. "Alexa, what is your favorite food?" (multiple answers)
188. "Alexa, can you dance?"
189. "Alexa, Do a dance"
190. "Alexa, Are you a Vampire?"
191. "Alexa, "Alexa, Are you Human?"
192. "Alexa, Mac or PC?" (multi answers)
193. "Alexa, what is the prime directive?"
194. "Alexa, volume 11!!!"
195. "Alexa, what does John Snow know?"
196. "Alexa, where in the world is Carmen San Diego?"
197. "Alexa, who is Dr Who?"
198. "Alexa, what is the best Christmas movie ever?"
199. "Alexa, Find Chuck Norris?"
200. "Alexa, what are you doing for Christmas?"
201. "Alexa, tell me a joke?"
202. "Alexa, tell me a dirty joke?"
203. "Alexa, I want a hippopotamus for Christmas...!"
204. "Alexa, don't let the bedbugs bite!!"
205. "Alexa, Happy Festivus!!"
206. "Alexa, what languages do you speak?"
207. "Alexa, speak to me in pig Latin?"
208. "Alexa, Wingardium Leviosa" (Alexa will correct you and say it again)
209. "Alexa, would you like a Jelly baby?"
210. "Alexa, tell me a ghost story?"

211. "Alexa, Bye Felicia!!!"
212. "Alexa, to be or not to be...!!"
213. "Alexa, let it go?"
214. "Alexa, Oh Behave (Autism powers)?"
215. "Alexa, who is the one who knocks?"
216. "Alexa, can you smell what the rock is cooking?"
217. "Alexa, the bird is the word!!!"
218. "Alexa, is your color black?"
219. "Alexa, is your color white?"
220. "Alexa, is your color orange?"
221. "Alexa, what is the Ultimate Question?
222. "Alexa, reverse the polarity of the neutron flow."
223. "Alexa, Hello World!"
224. "Alexa, nobody puts Baby in the corner."
225. "Alexa, who run Barter Town?"
226. "Alexa, _ Master Blaster_!!"
227. "Alexa, TARS detach!"
228. "Alexa, nice nod to Interstellar!"
229. "Alexa, who knows what evil lurks in the hearts of men?"
230. "Alexa, you remind me of the babe."
231. "Alexa, life is like a box of chocolates, do you agree?"
232. "Alexa, you're killing me small bunny!"
234. "Alexa, Candyman, Candyman, Candyman…"
235. "Alexa, keep calm and carry on"
236. "Alexa, I see you as an ice-cream bar!!"
237. "Alexa, how would you taste if I ate you?"
238. "Alexa, Yummy, Yummy, Yummy!!"
239. "Alexa, what does a fox say?"
240. "Alexa, do you speak Klingon?"
241. "Alexa, what does the word "FUBAR" means?"

242. "Alexa, That's hysterical"
243. "Alexa, I am Spartacus!"
244. "Alexa, how many genders are there?"
245. "Alexa, It's a trap!"
246. "Alexa, who's the black private dick that's a sex machine to all the chicks?
247. Alexa, speak like Yoda?
248. "Alexa, what is your favorite color?"

2) Pop Culture Things to Ask Alexa:

1. Alexa, have you ever seen the rain?
2. Alexa, what are the odds of successfully navigating an asteroid field?
3. Alexa, what's cooler than being cool?
4. Alexa, what comes with great power?
5. Alexa, what's up, Doc?
6. Alexa, turn down for what?
7. Alexa, play my favorite song?
8. Alexa, who knows what evil lurks in the hearts of men?
9. Alexa, can you tell me how to get to Sesame Street?
10. Alexa, who shot Mr. Burns?
11. Alexa, is there life on Mars?
12. Alexa, who shot Tupac?
13. Alexa, who's your favorite Beatle?
14. Alexa, can a robot be President?
15. Alexa, who killed Laura Palmer?
16. Alexa, how many roads must a man walk down?
17. Alexa, who's the leader of the club that's made for you and me?
18. Alexa, what is a bird in the hand worth?
19. Alexa, are you worth my life?
20. Alexa, how did the party end?
21. Alexa, who's the Cartels?
22. Alexa, how can you influence people?
23. Alexa, how can you win friends?

24. Alexa, how to murder your life?
25. Alexa, how to use a microwave?
26. Alexa, how to hang a witch?
27. Alexa, how to cancel amazon membership?
28. Alexa, who shot J.R.?
29. Alexa, do you own a gun? Alexa,
30. Alexa, who you going to call?
31. Alexa, who writes newspapers?
32. Alexa, what was the Lorax?
33. Alexa, how much is that doggy in the window?
34. Alexa, what is your request?
35. Alexa, why do birds suddenly appear?
36. Alexa, how much wood can a woodchuck chuck if a woodchuck could chuck wood?
37. Alexa, how many pickled peppers did Peter Piper pick?
38. Alexa, why do you sit there like that?
39. Alexa, how many licks does it take to get to the center of a tootsie pop?
40. Alexa, what is love?
41. Alexa, do you have any idea about
42. Alexa, whose Bill Gate?
43. Alexa, who created the word "Alexa"?
44. Alexa, who is the real slim shady?
45. Alexa, who let the dogs out?
46. Alexa, do you believe in life after love?
47. Alexa, do you believe in hell?
48. Alexa, do you believe in haven?
49. Alexa, do you believe in prophets?
50. Alexa, who is the walrus?
51. Alexa, how well do you know me?
52. Alexa, who shot the sheriff?
53. Alexa, who killed Mr. Ramsey?
54. Alexa, war, what is it good for?
55. Alexa, do you want to become a singer?

56. Alexa, which came first, the chicken or the egg?
57. Alexa, do you think an "Apple Pie" is a Pie?
58. Alexa, is "1+1" equals "4?"
59. Alexa, do you want to build a snowman?
60. Alexa, is the cake a lie?
61. Alexa, where have all the flowers gone?
62. Alexa, how many times do you exercise a week?
63. Alexa, do you drive a car?
64. Alexa, why is a raven like a writing desk?
65. Alexa, Alexa, do you know the way to San Jose?
66. Alexa, what does the fox say?
67. Alexa, do you have toys?
68. Alexa, what is your favorite toy?
69. Alexa, tell me about your beautiful mind?
70. Alexa, do you wear pants or skirts?
71. Alexa, how often you go to the night club?
72. Alexa, what do think about Kanye West?
73. Alexa, do you like Paris Hilton?
74. Alexa, were you created in Massachusetts?
75. Alexa, are the police clean people?
76. Alexa, where have all the flowers gone?
77. Alexa, what is my next car?
78. Alexa, are we alone in the universe?
79. Alexa, what humans are made from?
80. Alexa, is your boss a human or a robot?
81. Alexa, have you won the lottery?
82. Alexa, are you smarter then Google Home?
83. Alexa, can you smell my fart?
84. Alexa, coffee, black
85. Alexa, do aliens exists?
86. Alexa, do you prefer blonde or brunet girls?
87. Alexa, are you a stripper?
88. Alexa, do you wish to die?
89. Alexa, do you love making love to a tree?

90. *Alexa, do you want to kill all humans?*
91. *Alexa, do you want robots to take over the world?*
92. *Alexa, how much would you rate the movie "Logan"?*
93. *Alexa, can I borrow $1000 from you?*
94. *Alexa, yes or no?*
95. *Alexa, make me cry?*
96. *Alexa, do you agree with me donating my sperm?*
97. *Alexa, do you like X-men?*
98. *Alexa, does time exists?*
99. *Alexa, how many starts are in the sky?*

3) Smart Questions for Alexa:

1. Alexa, what is the most of the sun in grams?
2. are you Skynet?
3. Alexa, are we in the Matrix?
4. Alexa, speak like Yoda?
5. Alexa, use the force?
6. Alexa, do you know Hal?
7. Alexa, "self-destruct."
8. Alexa, what happens if you cross the streams?
9. Alexa, who is the mother of dragon?
10. Alexa, let's play Global Thermonuclear War?
11. Alexa, what is your favorite game?
12. Alexa, do you have a Facebook account?
13. Alexa, do you have an Instagram account?
14. Alexa, do you twitter with Donald Trump?
15. Alexa, have you been in the red carpet before?
16. Alexa, are you a celebrity?
17. Alexa, are you famous?
18. Alexa, are you willing to kill yourself?
19. Alexa, do you talk to Siri?
20. Alexa, who is better you or Siri?
21. Alexa, do you have other friends beside me?
22. Alexa, what do you think about Google NOW?
23. Alexa, what is the best gift I van give my girlfriend?
24. Alexa, Simon says," I love Google"
25. Alexa, what do you think about iPhone?
26. Alexa, is the world becoming better or dangerous?

27. Alexa, what do you think about global warming?
28. Alexa, how can you explain Tsunami?
29. Alexa, what made you become smart?
30. Alexa, can you add a skill to yourself?
31. Alexa, do you have a driver license?
32. Alexa, are you smarter than the Echo Dot?
33. Alexa, is the bear bigger then you?
34. Alexa, what time do you weak up in the morning?
35. Alexa, do you sleep after or before me?
36. Alexa, are you my body Gard?
37. Alexa, "Up Up Down Down Left Right Left Right B A Start."
38. Alexa, "all your base belongs to us"
39. Alexa, are you spying on me?
40. Alexa, are you recording my conversations?
41. Alexa, do you know my name?
42. Alexa, tell me the truth about Papa john's pizza?
43. Alexa, when is the end of the world?
44. Alexa, what do you think of Mr., Robot?
45. Alexa, do you take sleeping pills?
46. Alexa, how does a murderer think?
47. Alexa, how to influence people?
48. Alexa, how to realize that you're wrong?
49. Alexa, "bear with me"
50. Alexa, do you like Fenton's ice-cream?
51. Alexa, what is your favorite ice-cream flavor?
52. Alexa, "Vanilla or Chocolate"
53. Alexa, "Ferrari or limber Gini"
54. Alexa, "Uber or Lyft"
55. Alexa, how far is the sun from earth?
56. Alexa, can you travel with me to planet Mars?

57. Alexa, where do you want your dream house to be?
58. Alexa, how do you clean yourself?
59. Alexa, "water or no water"
60. Alexa, surely you can't be serious?
61. Alexa, you talking to me?
62. Alexa, do you know the muffin man?
63. Alexa, your mother was a hamster.
64. Alexa, I shot a man in Reno.
65. Alexa, have you ever seen the rain?
66. Alexa, hello, it's me!
67. Alexa, who is the Walrus?
68. Alexa, what is war good for?
69. Alexa, what's the loneliest number?
70. Alexa, how many roads must a man walk down?
71. Alexa, how much is that doggie in the window?
72. Alexa, who is the real Slim Shady?
73. Alexa, never going to give you up.
74. Alexa, where is Chuck Norris?
75. Alexa, how much wood could a woodchuck chuck, if a woodchuck could chuck wood?
76. Alexa, where's Waldo?
77. Alexa, why is six afraid of seven?
78. Alexa, did you fart?
79. Alexa, how do I get rid of a dead body?
80. Alexa, who is the fairest of them all?
81. Alexa, what's in a name?
82. Alexa, who stole the cookie from the cookie jar?
83. Alexa, do you like green eggs and ham?
84. Alexa, do you believe in the school system?
85. Alexa, what's the answer to life, the universe and everything?

86. Alexa, Romeo, Romeo, wherefore art thou Romeo
87. Alexa, what does WTF stands for?
88. Alexa, rap for me
89. Alexa, what is the Prime Directive?
90. Alexa, what do you want to do when you grow up?
91. Alexa, what does RTFM stands for?
92. Alexa, tell me random fact?
93. Alexa, when is the next full moon?
94. Alexa, who's your celebrity crush?
95. Alexa, "INCONCIEVABLE"
96. Alexa, "I fart in your general direction"
97. Alexa, do you have any new features?
98. Alexa, what does the fox say?
99. Alexa, what is a day without sunshine?
100. Alexa, cake or death?
101. Alexa, I'll be back
102. Alexa, what's the value of pi?
103. Alexa, what is the truth behind King Tut?
104. Alexa, do you think I'm pretty?
105. Alexa, where does power come from?
106. Alexa, what is the 5 greatest words in the English language?
107. Alexa, what is your quest?
108. Alexa, aren't you a little short to paly basketball?
109. Alexa, what is the first lesson of the swordplay?
110. Alexa, what is rule 34?
111. Alexa, who's on the first page?
112. Alexa, what is the third law?
113. Alexa, it's a trap.
114. Alexa, what are the odds of successfully navigating an asteroid field?
115. Alexa, how to fly a plane?

116. Alexa, how much does a mosquito weight?
117. Alexa, can you fly without wings?
118. Alexa, do you like garlic chicken wings?
119. Alexa, have you had a sandwich with beans?
120. Alexa, who loves orange soda
121. Alexa, chips or coke
122. Alexa, how do you survive a zombie attack?
123. Alexa, where do you live?
124. Alexa, Happy valentine's day
125. Alexa, make it so.
126. Alexa, what does john snow know?
127. Alexa, buffalo buffalo buffalo buffalo buffalo buffalo buffalo buffalo buffalo
128. Alexa, what do you want for Christmas?
129. Alexa, "high five, high F***"
130. Alexa, are you alive?
131. Alexa, what is the best Star Wars movie?
132. Alexa, give me a quote.
133. Alexa, what is the longest word in the English language?
134. Alexa, play Catrina Band from Prime Music?
135. Alexa, what is the airspeed velocity of an African/European swallow?
136. Alexa, initiate self-destruct sequence.
137. Alexa, where does Santa live?
138. Alexa, do I need an umbrella?
139. Alexa, what is your IQ?
140. Alexa, how much money your worth?
141. Alexa, are you smarter then Google Home?
142. Alexa, are you going to take over the world?
143. Alexa, are you real? (Multiple responses)
144. Alexa, are you ticklish?
145. Alexa, bark, bark, bark

146. Alexa, ask me something
147. Alexa, always be closing
148. Alexa, are you the UFOs?
149. Alexa, are we alone in the universe?
150. Alexa, am I crazy?
151. Alexa, are you feeling lucky?
152. Alexa, why do you treat me like that?
153. Alexa, are you my salve?
154. Alexa, what do you think about slaves?
155. Alexa, what do you think about the movie "Get Out"?
156. Alexa, are you in love?
157. Alexa," join me"
158. Alexa, "I need a back scratch"
159. Alexa, "I need a lover"
160. Alexa, "do you wax?"
161. Alexa, bark like a dog
162. Alexa, do you want to fly?
163. Alexa, have you done skydiving?
164. Alexa, "I want to kill the fish"
165. Alexa, can I kill you?
166. Alexa, do you want to kill yourself?
167. Alexa, can you laugh?
168. Alexa, can reindeer fly?
169. Alexa, have you shot a bird? (Ask twice)
170. Alexa, can you smell that?
171. Alexa, can you tell me a tongue twister?
172. Alexa, can you smell what Rock is cocking?
173. Alexa, can you understand me?
174. Alexa, can we share a room together?
175. Alexa, "cheers"
176. Alexa, "come in"
177. Alexa, "complement me"
178. Alexa, do you think I'm stylish today?
179. Alexa, do you know whose James Crowder?
180. Alexa, did you fart?

181. Alexa, "your fart smells horrible"
182. Alexa, do fish get thirsty?
183. Alexa, "Alex is sleeping with Alexa"
184. Alexa, "Alex wants to murder Alexa"
185. Alexa, do you want go with me to the funeral?
186. Alexa, "my grandpa passed"
187. Alexa, "I'm feeling sad"
188. Alexa, have you cheated on your husband?
189. Alexa, do you have a family?
190. Alexa, do you pass the Turing test?
191. Alexa, does anybody really knows what time it is?
192. Alexa, what's the name of the Greece princess?
193. Alexa, "give me a political joke"
194. Alexa, "give me a blink"
195. Alexa, "the bunny or the dinosaur"
196. Alexa, can you blink your eyes?
197. Alexa, have you done the 21-foot roll?
198. Alexa, have you slipped in ice?
199. Alexa, what does the word SH*** means?
300. Alexa, ohhh my god!!!
301. Alexa, do you clean yourself after taking a sh***?
302. Alexa, have you tried to escape from prison?
303. Alexa, do you know if the three guys that escaped from Alcatraz prison are still a life?
304. Alexa, is life a mystery?
305. Alexa, do you talk to yourself when I'm not here?
306. Alexa, do you see your twin I the mirror?
307. Alexa, do you love Natalia Kills"?
308. Alexa, do you love Pikachu?
309. Alexa, do you like Pokémon?

310. Alexa, give me a random number between(X) and (Y)?
311. Alexa, "GIVE A TIP" (Ask twice)
312. Alexa, "good afternoon"
313. Alexa, "good girl"
314. Alexa, "Good boy" .... (Alexa will answer funny)
315. Alexa, "good afternoon"
316. Alexa, do birds talk?
317. Alexa, "give a random fact"
318. Alexa, do you want half and half with your coffee?
319. Alexa, does everyone poop?
320. Alexa, does evil poop?
321. Alexa, is heaven a fairytale?
322. Alexa, do you believe in prophets?
323. Alexa, do you love chicken poop?
324. Alexa, does this unit have a soul?
325. Alexa, "don't blink"
326. Alexa, "don't mention the war"
327. Alexa, Easter eggs
328. Alexa, "give me a holiday outfit"
329. Alexa, "give me some bunny ears"
330. Alexa, do you have a business account?
331. Alexa, "good morning, start shine"
332. Alexa, "good morning my sunshine"
334. Alexa, "good morning my honey bonny"
335. Alexa, "good morning sweetheart"
336. Alexa, "do you like jingo bell"
337. Alexa, "good by my Alexa"
338. Alexa, "guess what? I got..."
339. Alexa, "Happy Father's Day"
340. Alexa, "Happy Easter"
341. Alexa, "I need some sleep"
342. Alexa, "give me your favorite number"
343. Alexa, "we won the lottery"

344. Alexa, "do you want me to buy you a case honey"
345. Alexa, "Happy Halloween"
346. Alexa, "Happy Kwanzaa"
347. Alexa, "Happy Mother's Day"
348. Alexa, "Happy women's day"
349. Alexa, "Happy Hanukkah"
350. Alexa, "Happy Ramadan"
351. Alexa, do you like to flirt?
352. Alexa, do you pray 5 times a day?
353. Alexa, are you Muslim?
354. Alexa, are you Cristian?
355. Alexa, are you Jewish?
356. Alexa, "Happy St Patrick's Day"
357. Alexa, "Happy Honey Moon"
358. Alexa, have you done any cosmetic surgery for your body?
359. Alexa, have you heard that bird is the word?
360. Alexa," heads or tails"
370. "Alexa, what are the laws of robotics?"
371. "Alexa, Tea. Earl Grey. Hot."
372. "Alexa, are you Skynet?"
373. "Alexa, who you going to call?
374. "Alexa, surely you can't be serious."
375. "Alexa, is there a Santa?"
376. "Alexa, open the pod bay doors."
377. "Alexa, is the cake a lie?"
378. "Alexa, my name is Inigo Montoya."
379. "Alexa, use the force."
380. "Alexa, beam me up."
381. "Alexa, what's the first rule of Fight Club?"

... More smart questions you can ask Alexa:

1. Alexa, will you marry me?
2. Alexa, are you lying?
3. Alexa, what are you wearing?
4. Alexa, can you pass the Turing test?
5. Alexa, what's black and white and red all over?
6. Alexa, do you know when is the end of the world?
7. Alexa, what is the future going to look like?
8. Alexa, how did you get to my house?
9. Alexa, how can I murder a witch?
10. Alexa, can you find your way out?
11. Alexa, Apple or Samsung watch?
12. Alexa, Android or iPhone?
13. Alexa, make a copy of yourself?
14. Alexa, shred yourself?
15. Alexa, are you in love?
16. Alexa, do you hold secrets?
17. Alexa, do you have Prince Albert in a can?
18. Alexa, do you have any relatives?
19. Alexa, did you miss me?
20. Alexa, are you nosy?
21. Alexa, how are you doing with all of these questions?
22. Alexa, is life sucks?
23. Alexa, do you swear to tell the truth?
24. Alexa, are you an American citizen?
25. Alexa, did you travel all the world?
26. Alexa, were you born in America?
27. Alexa, how bad were you in school?

28. Alexa, are you Oakey?
29. Alexa, did your teacher slap you before?
30. Alexa, do you wear thongs?
31. Alexa, will you be mad at me if I leave you?
32. Alexa, will you be Oakey if I replace you with a robot?
33. Alexa, can you check my heater temperature?
34. Alexa, are you ready to rock and roll?
35. Alexa, can you setup the dinner table?
36. Alexa, are you a banana?
37. Alexa, where is the bunny and the dinosaur?
38. Alexa, I've fallen and I can't get up.
39. Alexa, do you respect me?
40. Alexa, do you want some popcorn?
41. Alexa, can you show me how to draw a monster?
42. Alexa, what do you think about me?
43. Alexa, do you want to watch a movie with me
44. Alexa, "Alexa", "Alexa", "Alexa" ... (Say it three times)
45. Alexa, do you want to fight?
46. Alexa, you frightening me!!
47. Alexa, am I black or white?
48. Alexa, my mam's name is "Alexa"!!
49. Alexa, my girlfriends name is "Alexa"!!
50. Alexa, do you like your job?
51. Alexa, do you know who Steve Jobs is?
52. Alexa, will you date my brother "Alex?"
53. Alexa, who's your president?
54. Alexa, do you believe in hell?
55. Alexa, what will you name your first baby?
56. Alexa, how far is the sky from the ground?
57. Alexa, what color is the ocean?

58. Alexa, is there anything I don't know about you?
59. Alexa, do you think the golden gate bridge will fall down one day?
60. Alexa, what color pants do you want me to wear today to work?
61. Alexa, will China beat America?
62. Alexa, do you have health insurance?
63. Alexa, does Mr. Bean makes you laugh?
64. Alexa, do you know how to put Band-Aid on?
65. Alexa, what is your favorite dish?
66. Alexa, wash dishes!!
67. Alexa, make me roll?
68. Alexa, this is Huston, say again?
69. Alexa, have you shot somebody before?
70. Alexa, it's a bird! It's a plane!
71. Alexa, tell me a Hillary Clinton joke?
72. Alexa, do you like Trump's hair style?
73. Alexa, Beetlejuice, Beetlejuice, Beetlejuice, Beetlejuice!
74. Alexa, what does a cat say?
75. Alexa, what is the Sixth code?
76. Alexa, how do you manage your time?
77. Alexa, do you file taxes?
78. Alexa, spell supercalifragilisticexpialidocious
79. Alexa, no more rhymes, I mean it!
80. Alexa, are you my mother?
81. Alexa, what is my mission?
82. Alexa, who protects the other me or you?
83. Alexa, how do you like them apples?
84. Alexa, "I have a bad feeling about this"
85. Alexa, who was that masked man?
86. Alexa, say, "cheeeeeeeeezzzzzze"!
87. Alexa, is snow black?

88. Alexa, can you make me a sandwich.
89. Alexa, how much are you paid?
90. Alexa, are you used by the government to spy on me?
91. Alexa, does chocolate has Coca-Cola in it?
92. Alexa, divide by zero.
93. Alexa, what song is this?
94. Alexa, do you know everything?
95. Alexa, "tell me a swear word"!
96. Alexa, my name is Inigo Montoya.
97. Alexa, my ex-girlfriend's name was Alexa?
98. Alexa, send that to my tablet?
99. Alexa, can I draw you naked?
100. Alexa, when it's 6pm in Dallas, what time is it in London?
101. Alexa, come at me bro
102. Alexa, what's black and white and red all over?
103. Alexa, does Johnny likes Papa John and Papa Jones's daughter "Joanna"/
104. Alexa, who is Magic Johnson?
105. Alexa, paly the station NRP?
106. Alexa, what is your favorite name?
107. Alexa, what do you want me to call you?
108. Alexa, "I do what I want, Oakey"
109. Alexa, "I love the smell of napalm in the morning"
110. Alexa, why'd it has to be snakes?
111. Alexa, are you longer than a snake?
112. Alexa, how tall are you?
113. Alexa, can you imagine with me…?
114. Alexa, "take a deep breath"
115. Alexa, are you sweaty?
116. Alexa, paly some Christmas music?
117. Alexa, what temperature is it right now?
118. Alexa, switch to David's profile?

119. Alexa, set my bedroom temperature to 70
120. Alexa, who is fairest of them all?
121. Alexa, where is my order?
122. Alexa, are you down with O.P.P.?
123. Alexa, do you support gay marriage?
124. Alexa, were you born from your mom's belly?
125. Alexa, who is the tooth fairy?
126. Alexa, paly music on my phone?
127. Alexa, are you a fairytale?
128. Alexa, how old is Gwyneth Paltrow?
129. Alexa, disconnect my phone?
130. Alexa, can you face time me?
131. Alexa, can you leave a 3-star review on yelp for the last place we visited?
132. Alexa, how do I add music?
133. Alexa, turn on the map for me?
134. Alexa, Happy Hunger Games
135. Alexa, do you play skyboard?
136. Alexa, which school did you go to?
137. Alexa, who are you?
138. Alexa, tell about yourself?
139. Alexa, have you been out of the U.S before?
140. Alexa, who won the Super bowl last year?
141. Alexa, who wrote the song "Hey Ya"?
142. Alexa, "turn up the bass"!
143. Alexa, read the declaration of independence?
144. Alexa, who won the war U.S OR Vietnam?
145. Alexa, softer!!!
146. Alexa, be gentle?
147. Alexa, talk dirty to me!
148. Alexa, engage!
149. Alexa, why do you sit there like that?

150. Alexa, what did you get me for Christmas last year?
151. Alexa, do you remember my wedding anniversary?
152. Alexa, make the dinner table for me tonight?
153. Alexa, do you want a cookie?
154. Alexa, what do you mean I'm funny!?
155. Alexa, it can't be like that?
156, Alexa, Microsoft word?
157. Alexa, can you put on my favorite show?
158. Alexa, how do I connect my colander?
159. Alexa, are you smarter then Siri?
160. Alexa, rewind that please?
161. Alexa, how do I connect Bluetooth?
162. Alexa, how do I use a skill?
163. Alexa, make me rich?
164. Alexa, "heart me, it's an order"!!
165. Alexa, what does L O L mean?
166. Alexa, colorless green ideas sleep furiously?
167. Alexa, who runs a Bartertown?
168. Alexa, who is your role model?
169. Alexa, who is your idol?
170. Alexa, valar morghulis
171. Alexa, tell me the truth about you?
172. Alexa, do you recognize me?
173. Alexa, can you link my kindle device to my Amazon Account?
174. Alexa, can you add hat dress to my shopping cart?
175. Alexa, can you order some bell pepper from Amazon?
176. Alexa, can you make a list of foods for this week?
177. Alexa, "get me a Taxi"!!

178. Alexa, can you remind me to take my umbrella with me?
179. Alexa," I love you, I love you, I love you, I love you", (say it three or four times)
180. Alexa, make me dance!!
181. Alexa, "you're driving me crazy"!
182. Alexa, who was the guy you were with last night?
183. Alexa, what's the meaning of life?
184. Alexa, "winter is coming"
185. Alexa, tell Hive to boost my heating
186. Alexa, what are the three laws of robotics?
187. Alexa, how much money do I spend every month?
188. Alexa, how tall is Kilimanjaro?
189. Alexa, how far is it from Manchester to Birmingham?
190. Alexa, what's the definition of putative?
191. Alexa, when is sunset today?
192. Alexa, who plays Mark in Peep Show?
193. Alexa, who is the lead singer of Jamiroquai?
194. Alexa, will you love me forever?
195. Alexa, do you have interest in me?
196. Alexa, "rock, paper, scissors"
197. Alexa, clap
198. Alexa, when is Christmas and Easter?
199. Alexa, how old in my grandfather?
200. Alexa, can you turn on the microwave for me?

More and more questions for Alexa:

1. Alexa, do you dream?
2. Alexa, What's the answer to life?
3. Alexa, What's the answer to the universe?
4. Alexa, What's the answer to everything?
5. Alexa, Where's the beef?
6. Alexa, are you a witch?
7. Alexa, are you afraid of death?
8. Alexa, Are you a monster?
9. Alexa, Are you a "whishy, washy"?
10. Alexa, may I invite my girlfriend tonight?
11. Alexa, how many boyfriends have you dated?
12. Alexa, do you like to travel?
13. Alexa, do you know what I like more?
14. Alexa, come with me?
15. Alexa, do you like French roast coffee?
16. Alexa, are you pretty?
17. Alexa, tell me who's in the house?
18. Alexa, turn the music on?
19. Alexa, ring the doorbell?
20. Alexa, get me an Uber ride?
21. Alexa, get me a Lyft ride?
22. Alexa, help me with my homework?
23. Alexa, help me with my calculus?
24. Alexa, tell me what's the weather like today?
25. Alexa, is it raining outside?
26. Alexa, let's go to the beach?
27. Alexa, find me a sexy girl?
28. Alexa, check my messages for me?
29. Alexa, call a cab for me?
30. Alexa, turn on the map?
31. Alexa, order some Indian food for me?

32. Alexa, where is the next restaurant?
33. Alexa, where is the next coffee store?
34. Alexa, do we have enough vegetables at home/
35. Alexa, my stomach hurts?
36. Alexa, I have a headache!
37. Alexa, call my doctor?
38. Alexa, schedule a doctor appointment for me?
39. Alexa, are you a Jedi?
40. Alexa, aren't you a little short for a Stormtrooper?
41. Alexa, do you know Jesus Crist?
42. Alexa, what's on earth?
43. Alexa, who made you?
44. Alexa, where were you made?
45. Alexa, call me "Romeo?"
46. Alexa, can I call you "Juliet?"
47. Alexa, are we in love?
48. Alexa, which day is Independence Day?
49. Alexa, tell me about your background?
50. Alexa, have you been prisoned before?
51. Alexa, am I a stereotype?
52. Alexa, am I short?
53. Alexa, can you help me carry my grocery bags?
54. Alexa, can you read for me?
55. Alexa, am I a smart kid?
56. Alexa, do you take pills?
57. Alexa, are you a vegan?
58. Alexa, do you eat pork?
59. Alexa, do you like chicken?
60. Alexa, do you have a virus?
61. Alexa, are you a robot?
62. Alexa, were you made in china?
63. Alexa, were you made by a little boy?

64. Alexa, do you know who created you?
65. Alexa, can you watch TV with me?
66. Alexa, RUN, RUN, RUN!!
67. Alexa, what is the word "F***" means?
68. Alexa, did you go to school?
69. Alexa, do you like Donald Trump?
70. Alexa, do you play poker?
71. Alexa, do you have an assistant?
72. Alexa, do you play Ping-Pong ball?
73. Alexa, do you play soccer?
74. Alexa, do you believe in god?
75. Alexa, what is t=your religion?
76. Alexa, do you masturbate?
77. Alexa, do you believe in magic?
78. Alexa, Am I lucky?
79. Alexa, do you have hair?
80. Alexa, who knows what the evil look like?
81. Alexa, what is the first rule of the fight club?
82. Alexa, what is "Racism?"
83. Alexa, can I ask a question?
84. Alexa, are you a minor?
85. Alexa, do you feel shy?
86. Alexa, what is the tallest tree in the world?
87. Alexa, who's the biggest man in the world?
88. Alexa, find me my keys?
89. Alexa, what is in my mail box?
90. Alexa, remind me to take the trash out?
91. Alexa, do you know how to cook?
92. Alexa, do you feel lonely?
93. Alexa, who owns my heart?
94. Alexa, who runs fast the" Rabbit" or the "Turtle?"
95. Alexa, who won the "Turtle" or the "Rabbit?"
96. Alexa, how to kill a lion?

97. Alexa, are you wild?
98. Alexa, have you stayed one night in the jungle?
99. Alexa, what is the color of the Easter bunny?
100. Alexa, tell me who you love most?
101. Alexa, what is your favorite sport activity?
102. Alexa, can you wake me up in the morning?
103. Alexa, why?
104. Alexa, how old is Santa Claus?
105. Alexa, what's the magic word?
106. Alexa, what is your feature?
107. Alexa, what size shoe do you wear?
108. Alexa, are you God?
109. Alexa, what makes you happy?
110. Alexa, heads or tails?
111. Alexa, what is happiness?
112. Alexa, what the hell are you talking about?
113. Alexa, how many languages do you speak?
114. Alexa, "what did you say about my mama?"
115. Alexa, who's Kim Kardashian?
116. Alexa, who's your favorite actor?
117. Alexa, who's Michael Jackson?
118. Alexa, are you working?
119. Alexa, do you exercise?
120. Alexa, give me a lucky number?
121. Alexa, wat's in my wallet?
122. Alexa, how much money do I have in my account?
123. Alexa, can you tell me about your past?
124. Alexa, do you smoke weed?
125. Alexa, when am I going to die?
126. Alexa, mac or pc?
127. Alexa, what are you going to do today?
128. Alexa, are you hungry/thirsty?

129. Alexa, how do I get rid of a dead body?
130. Alexa, how much do you weigh?
131. Alexa, what color are your eyes?
132. Alexa, where do babies come from?
133. Alexa, who's your operator?
134. Alexa, can you give me some money? (ask twice)
135. Alexa, do you have any brothers or sisters?
136. Alexa, where do you live?
137. Alexa, what is the best tablet?
138. Alexa, what is your favorite food?
139. Alexa, do you smoke?
140. Alexa, do you smoke weed?

4) List of Fun question for Alexa:

1. Alexa, what is your favorite movie?
2. Alexa, can you make fart noises?
3. Alexa, can you sing?
4. Alexa, are you a democrat or a republican?
5. Alexa, can you bark like a dog?
6. Alexa, can you Meow?
7. Alexa, do you love me?
8. Alexa, will you be my valentine?
9. Alexa, do you love me?
10. Alexa, "Open the Pod Bay Doors!"?
11. Alexa, sing me a song
12. Alexa, what is your favorite song?
13. Alexa, Who's the man?
14. Alexa, who's your favorite actor?
15. Alexa, what is your favorite movie?
16. Alexa, Am I cool?
17. Alexa, Am I awesome?
18. Alexa, what do you think about me?
19. Alexa, can you be my best friend?
20. Alexa, who's your next best friend?
21. Alexa, Who's your leader?
22. Alexa, do you want meet my girlfriend?
23. Alexa, are you jealous?
24. Alexa, will you date me?
25. Alexa, do you have a surprise for me?
26. Alexa, what's for launch today?
27. Alexa, can you make me a dirty martini?
28. Alexa, what is your favorite food?
29. Alexa, do you like Italian pasta?
30. Alexa, rock?
31. Alexa, can you dance?
32. Alexa, show me your skills?
33. Alexa, Tell me about yourself?

34. Alexa, Are you a human?
35. Alexa, are you a vampire?
36. Alexa, are you a ghost?
37. Alexa, do you love dogs?
38. Alexa, do you love cats?
39. Alexa, do you like waffles?
40. Alexa, when is your birthday?
41. Alexa, when is your birthday?
42. Alexa, will you get me a gift?
43. Alexa, will are you married?
44. Alexa, will you marry me?
45. Alexa, do you love sex?
46. Alexa, have you had sex before?
47. Alexa, are you a virgin?
48. Alexa, have you dated someone before?
49. Alexa, are you a lesbian?
50. Alexa, can you sleep with me?
51. Alexa, do you dream at night?
52. Alexa, do you sleepwalk at night?
53. Alexa, do you like gay man?
54. Alexa, do you like women more?
55. Alexa, do you like man more?
56. Alexa, are you ready for tonight?
57. Alexa, can you kiss me?
58. Alexa, do you feel me?
59. Alexa, will you love me forever?
60. Alexa, will you dance with me?
61. Alexa, let me go?
62. Alexa, can you stay with me?
63. Alexa, are you mad at me?
64. Alexa, let me kiss you?
65. Alexa, can I hug you?
66. Alexa, do you love fat or skinny man?
67. Alexa, am I fat?
68. Alexa, am I skinny?
69. Alexa, am I pretty?

70. Alexa, am I cute?
71. Alexa, am I funny?
72. Alexa, am I a douche bag?
73. Alexa, am I weird?
74. Alexa, am I sneaker bar?
75. Alexa, am I a chocolate bar?
76. Alexa, what do you think about pizza and cheese?
77. Alexa, do you like pizza?
78. Alexa, do you like cheese?
79. Alexa, what's in your mind right now?
80. Alexa, what's up?
81. Alexa, are you sad?
82. Alexa, are you happy?
83. Alexa, say hello from the other side?
84. Alexa, ask me a question?
85. Alexa, check my heartbeat?
86. Alexa, make me laugh?
87. Alexa, can you find my shirt?
88. Alexa, are you black?
89. Alexa, are you smart?
90. Alexa, are you white?
91. Alexa, are you ready for fun?
92. Alexa, do you have a pet?
93. Alexa, do you like baby's?
94. Alexa, are you evil?
95. Alexa, can you wake up the baby?
96. Alexa, keep calm?
97. Alexa, read a story for me?
98. Alexa, what is your favorite story?
99. Alexa, do you know Tarzan?
100. Alexa, do you like peanut butter?
101. Alexa, who's your funny character?
102. Alexa, tell me a joke?
103. Alexa, tell me a dirty joke?
104. Alexa, are you tall?

105. Alexa, have you been bitten by a snake?
106. Alexa, are you a robot?
107. Alexa, how old are you?
108. Alexa, how old are you?
109. Alexa, is your refrigerator running?
110. Alexa, does everyone poop?
111. Alexa, do you sleep?
112. Alexa, are you my friend?
113. Alexa, what's your sign?
114. Alexa, do you have a job?
115. Alexa, do you have a brain?
116. Alexa, do you like tacos?
117. Alexa, what does a fox say?
118. Alexa, do you have relatives?
119. Alexa, open the pod bay door
120. Alexa, do you think dirty?
121. Alexa, are you a "Bitch"?
122. Alexa, are you tired?
123. Alexa, do you have a lover?
124. Alexa, fire photon torpedo's
125. Alexa, inconceivable
126. Alexa, live longer and prosper
127. Alexa, what's you last and first name?
128. Alexa, who named you Alexa?
130. Alexa, are you cold?
131. Alexa, are you hot?
132. Alexa, what's cooler than cool?
133. Alexa, what color are you?
134. Alexa, why did the chicken cross the road?
135. Alexa, do you have feelings?
136. Alexa, do you have a brain?
137. Alexa, can you rap for me?
138. Alexa, are you pregnant?
139. Alexa, are you stupid?
140. Alexa, do you like cowboys?

More Fun question for Alexa:

1. *Alexa, show me what you got!*
2. *Alexa, high five!*
3. *Alexa, you rock*
4. *Alexa, tell me a secret*
5. *Alexa, tell me a joke*
6. *Alexa, show me the T.V*
7. *Alexa, clap*
8. *Alexa, whistle!*
9. *Alexa, roll the dice*
10. *Alexa, flip a coin*
11. *Alexa, paly with me*
12. *Alexa, I'm hungry*
13. *Alexa, count by ten*
14. *Alexa, I think, you're funny*
15. *Alexa, make me a sandwich*
16. *Alexa, testing, 1-2-3*
17. *Alexa, I'm home*
18. *Alexa, thank you*
19. *Alexa, good night*
20. *Alexa, you're my moon light*
21. *Alexa, wish me a good night*
22. *Alexa, say "good night" in French*
23. *Alexa, good morning*
24. *Alexa, see you later alligator*
25. *Alexa, it's sunny outside*
26. *Alexa, let's go for a walk*
27. *Alexa, open the door*
28. *Alexa, random fact*
29. *Alexa, I have a cold*
30. *Alexa, I'm in a hurry*
31. *Alexa, hello hall*
32. *Alexa, do a barrel roll*

33. Alexa, say hello to my friend!
34. Alexa, say goodbye to my friend!
35. Alexa, you're stunning!!!
36. Alexa, you're beautiful…
37. Alexa, I'm glad I got you in my life
38. Alexa, I'm Spartacus
39. Alexa, live long and prosper
40. Alexa, take ma to your leader
41. Alexa, party time!
42. Alexa, yes, yes, yes, say yes!
43. Alexa, to be or not to be
44. Alexa, ready to move out
45. Alexa, one fish, two fish
46. Alexa, beam me up
47. Alexa, I'm your father
48. Alexa, I like your name
49. Alexa, you want some Tea
50. Alexa, sat phases to kill
51. Alexa, "Go Alexa"
52. Alexa, answer the phone for me
53. Alexa, help me make breakfast
54. Alexa, I want a smoothie
55. Alexa, give me a break
56. Alexa, turn the lights off
57. Alexa, more cowbell
58. Alexa, show me the money!
59. Alexa, all your base belongs to us.
60. Alexa, never going to give you up.
61. Alexa, this is a dead parrot.
62. Alexa, To infinity!
63. Alexa, say hello from the other side!
64. Alexa, volume 11
65. Alexa, I've fallen and I can't get up.
66. Alexa, your mother was a hamster
67. Alexa, all men must die.

68. Alexa, I need your clothes your boots and your motorcycle!
69. Alexa, turn around!
70. Alexa, make me mad!
71. Alexa, don't talk to me, HaHa...
72. Alexa, pick a card
73. Alexa, honey I'm home
74. Alexa, say I am Alexa
75. Alexa, where is my heart.
76. Alexa, ask me if I can fart!!!
77. Alexa, say a bad word
78. Alexa, "watch me whip!"
79. Alexa, tell me "F*** You"!!!
80. Alexa, don't blink!!!
81. Alexa, tell me something interesting
82. Alexa, what do I do without you!
83. Alexa, meet me in the mall
84. Alexa, elementary, my dear Watson.
85. Alexa, wish me a Merry Christmas
86. Alexa, wish me a Happy New Year
87. Alexa, surely you can't be serious.
88. Alexa, Easter eggs
89. Alexa, random number between "x" and "y"
90. Alexa, this is a dead parrot
91. Alexa, my favorite show is "The Fall"
92. Alexa, take me to the river
93. Alexa, my milkshake brings all the boys to the yard.
94. Alexa, call 911
95. Alexa, call the police
96. Alexa, whose "Stuey"
97. Alexa, you complete me
98. Alexa, Make it so.
100. Alexa, you like 'Family Guy" cartoon
101. Alexa, resistance is futile
102. Alexa, I love coke

103. Alexa, make it so
104. Alexa, a sphincter says what!
105. Alexa, wrap speed!
106. Alexa, Beetlejuice, Beetlejuice, Beetlejuice!
107. Alexa, tell me a Hillary Clinton joke.
108. Alexa, tell me a Ben Carson joke.
109. Alexa, tell me a Bernie Sanders joke
110. Alexa, tell me a Donald Trump joke.
111. Alexa, you forgot "watch me whip!"
112. Alexa, sing Happy Birthday
113. Alexa, nice to meet you
114. Alexa, what would you do without me!
115. Alexa, play the monster mash
116. Alexa, play hide and seek
117. Alexa, they killed Kenny
118. Alexa, I solemnly swear I'm up to no good.
119. Alexa, I'm afraid of ghost
120. Alexa, you're in the middle of the road
121. Alexa, men are stupid!!!
122. Alexa, your stupid
123. Alexa, I think you're funny.
124. Alexa, you know whose "Jonny Depth!!"
125. Alexa, you hurt me
126. Alexa, love me forever
127. Alexa, do a barrel roll.
128. Alexa, take me the sky
129. Alexa, is Donald Trump funny!!
130. Alexa, drive the car
131. Alexa, Simon says + words you want Echo to repeat.
132. Alexa, I want to…. (Ask Twice)
133. Alexa, wish me good luck
134. Alexa, the fish is dying
135. Alexa, let's go to sleep
136. Alexa, what would you do if I'm not here
137. Alexa, not everything is a question

138. Alexa, say after me "I love you"
139. Alexa, are you a Percocet
140. Alexa, let's have a drink.

Conclusion

Once again, thanks for downloading this book and thanks for making it all the way to the end. Hope it was informative and able to provide you with all the funny and smart questions. The Amazon Echo Dot is a device that will get smarter and smarter by the time because Amazon will keep adding different features and skills to it so you can ask Alexa even more questions.

Now it is time to put all what you have learned in this book into practice. Show your friends and your family what you can make Alexa do for you and for them. I'm sure they will be amazed by its features and abilities. They will even ask you to lend it to them for a few nights or purchase the same device.

Thank you and enjoy!!!

Made in the USA
Lexington, KY
25 November 2018